The Power of Personal Accountability:
Taking Control of Your Life

Eithan Drew

Copyright © [2023]

Title: The Power of Personal Accountability: Taking Control of Your Life
Author's: Eithan Drew

This book was printed and published by [Publisher's: **Eithan Drew**] in [2023]

ISBN:

TABLE OF CONTENT

Chapter 1: Understanding Personal Accountability

The Importance of Personal Accountability

Recognizing the Benefits of Taking Responsibility for Your Actions

Common Barriers to Personal Accountability

Chapter 2: Developing a Mindset of Personal Accountability

Cultivating Self-Awareness

Owning Your Choices and Decisions

Overcoming the Fear of Failure and Success

Chapter 3: Taking Responsibility for Your Actions

Acknowledging Your Mistakes

Learning from Failures and Moving Forward

Accepting Consequences and Making Amends

Chapter 4: Building Personal Accountability in Relationships 26

Taking Responsibility for Your Role in Relationships

Communicating Effectively and Resolving Conflicts

Holding Yourself Accountable in Collaborative Efforts

Chapter 5: Personal Accountability in the Workplace 32

Understanding Your Role and Responsibilities

Setting Clear Goals and Expectations

Taking Initiative and Demonstrating Accountability

Chapter 6: Overcoming Procrastination and Building Discipline 38

Identifying the Root Causes of Procrastination

Strategies for Overcoming Procrastination

Cultivating Discipline and Consistency

Chapter 1: Understanding Personal Accountability

The Importance of Personal Accountability

In our fast-paced and ever-changing world, it is easy to get caught up in the chaos and lose sight of the importance of personal accountability. However, taking responsibility for our actions is crucial for achieving personal growth and success in all aspects of life. Whether it is in our relationships, careers, or personal development, personal accountability is the foundation upon which we can build a fulfilling and purposeful life.

Taking responsibility for our actions means acknowledging that we have the power to shape our own destinies. It means recognizing that our choices and decisions have consequences and that we are responsible for the outcomes we experience. When we accept personal accountability, we empower ourselves to take control of our lives and make the necessary changes to improve our circumstances.

One of the key benefits of personal accountability is the ability to learn from our mistakes. By accepting responsibility for our actions, we can reflect on our choices and behaviors, identify areas for improvement, and make the necessary adjustments to avoid repeating the same mistakes in the future. This self-reflection and willingness to learn and grow are essential for personal development and achieving long-term success.

Moreover, personal accountability fosters trust and credibility in our relationships. When we demonstrate that we are reliable, trustworthy, and willing to take ownership of our actions, others are more likely to respect and trust us. This opens up opportunities for deeper connections, collaboration, and growth in both personal and professional relationships.

Additionally, personal accountability gives us a sense of control over our lives. Rather than feeling like victims of circumstances, we become active participants in creating our own realities. By taking responsibility for our actions, we shift our mindset from one of blame and excuses to one of empowerment and possibility. This mindset shift allows us to overcome challenges, persevere in the face of adversity, and achieve our goals.

In conclusion, personal accountability is the cornerstone of personal growth and success. By taking responsibility for our actions, we can learn from our mistakes, build trust in our relationships, and regain control over our lives. It is a powerful mindset that empowers us to shape our own destinies and create the life we desire. So, let us embrace personal accountability and take control of our lives today. Remember, we have the power to make a difference, and it all starts with taking responsibility for our own actions.

Recognizing the Benefits of Taking Responsibility for Your Actions

In today's society, it is all too common for people to deflect blame and make excuses for their actions. However, the power of personal accountability cannot be underestimated. Taking responsibility for your actions is not only a sign of maturity but also a key ingredient to success and personal growth.

When you take responsibility for your actions, you are acknowledging that you have control over your life. This mindset empowers you to make positive changes and take proactive steps towards achieving your goals. Instead of dwelling on past mistakes or blaming others, you can focus on finding solutions and improving yourself.

One of the greatest benefits of taking responsibility for your actions is the ability to learn and grow from your experiences. By accepting responsibility, you can reflect on your actions, identify areas for improvement, and make necessary changes. This self-reflection helps you avoid repeating the same mistakes and enables personal growth and development.

Furthermore, taking responsibility for your actions builds trust and credibility with others. When you own up to your mistakes and take the necessary steps to rectify them, people around you will see you as reliable and trustworthy. This can lead to more meaningful relationships, both personally and professionally.

Taking responsibility for your actions also promotes a positive and proactive mindset. Instead of feeling like a victim or being at the mercy of circumstances, you become the driver of your own life. This mindset allows you to approach challenges with resilience and determination, knowing that you have the power to overcome any obstacles.

In addition, personal accountability fosters a sense of ownership and pride in your work. When you take responsibility for your actions, you are more likely to put in the effort and strive for excellence. This dedication can lead to greater success in your career and personal endeavors.

Ultimately, recognizing the benefits of taking responsibility for your actions is crucial for personal growth, success, and overall well-being. By embracing personal accountability, you can take control of your life, learn from your mistakes, build trust with others, develop a proactive mindset, and achieve your goals. So, take a moment to reflect on your actions and start taking responsibility today. Your future self will thank you.

Common Barriers to Personal Accountability

Introduction:
In our journey to take control of our lives, one of the essential steps is embracing personal accountability. By acknowledging that we are responsible for our actions and choices, we empower ourselves to make positive changes and create the life we desire. However, there are common barriers that often hinder our ability to fully embrace personal accountability. In this subchapter, we will explore these obstacles and discover ways to overcome them, enabling us to take responsibility for our actions.

1.   Fear   of   Failure:
One of the most prevalent barriers to personal accountability is the fear of failure. Many individuals are afraid to take responsibility for their actions because they worry about making mistakes or facing negative outcomes. However, it is crucial to understand that failure is a natural part of growth and learning. Embrace the mindset that failure is an opportunity to learn and improve.

2.   Blaming   Others:
Blaming others is another significant barrier to personal accountability. It is easy to shift responsibility onto external factors or other individuals instead of taking ownership of our actions. However, true personal growth comes from accepting our mistakes and learning from them. Recognize that blaming others only hinders our progress and prevents us from taking control of our lives.

3.   Lack   of   Self-Awareness:
A lack of self-awareness can also hinder personal accountability.

Without understanding our own strengths, weaknesses, and values, it becomes challenging to take responsibility for our actions. Developing self-awareness through reflection and introspection allows us to identify areas where we need improvement and take the necessary steps towards personal growth.

4.   Procrastination:
Procrastination is a barrier that affects many individuals when it comes to personal accountability. Putting off tasks or actions prevents us from taking responsibility and can lead to feelings of guilt and dissatisfaction. Overcome procrastination by breaking tasks into smaller, manageable steps, setting clear deadlines, and holding yourself accountable to complete them.

5.   Fear   of   Change:
Lastly, the fear of change often hinders personal accountability. Change can be uncomfortable and challenging, but it is necessary for growth and progress. Embrace change as an opportunity for personal development and be willing to step outside your comfort zone. Remember that personal accountability is rooted in taking ownership of your actions and embracing change is an essential part of that process.

Conclusion:
Recognizing and overcoming these common barriers to personal accountability is crucial for taking control of our lives. By addressing the fear of failure, avoiding blame, developing self-awareness, combating procrastination, and embracing change, we can break free from the constraints that hinder our personal growth. Taking responsibility for our actions empowers us to create the life we desire,

fostering a sense of fulfillment and accomplishment. So, let go of these barriers and embrace personal accountability to unlock your true potential.

Chapter 2: Developing a Mindset of Personal Accountability

Cultivating Self-Awareness

In the journey of personal growth and development, there is one skill that stands out as the foundation for all others: self-awareness. The ability to understand oneself, recognize our strengths and weaknesses, and take responsibility for our actions is the first step towards taking control of our lives. In this subchapter, we will explore the importance of cultivating self-awareness and how it can empower every individual to embrace personal accountability.

Taking responsibility for our actions is not always an easy task. Often, we find ourselves blaming external factors or other people for our failures and shortcomings. However, true personal accountability starts with self-reflection and an honest assessment of our own behaviors and decisions. Cultivating self-awareness allows us to break free from the cycle of blame and excuses, and instead, take ownership of our lives.

Self-awareness is a journey of self-discovery. It involves deep introspection and a willingness to confront our fears, insecurities, and limiting beliefs. By examining our thoughts, emotions, and patterns of behavior, we gain a clearer understanding of who we are and what drives us. This awareness then becomes a powerful tool for personal growth, as it allows us to identify areas for improvement and make conscious choices that align with our values and goals.

Furthermore, self-awareness enhances our relationships with others. When we are aware of our own actions and their impact on those around us, we become more empathetic and understanding. We begin to recognize that our words and behaviors have consequences, and we can take steps to ensure that our actions are aligned with our intentions. By taking responsibility for our actions, we foster healthier and more authentic connections with others, built on trust and mutual respect.

In conclusion, cultivating self-awareness is fundamental to taking control of our lives and embracing personal accountability. It empowers us to break free from the cycle of blame, excuses, and victimhood, and instead, take ownership of our actions. By understanding ourselves better, we can identify areas for improvement, make conscious choices, and foster healthier relationships. Whether you are a student, a professional, or a parent, the power of self-awareness is relevant to everyone. Start your journey towards self-discovery today and unlock your full potential.

Owning Your Choices and Decisions

In the journey of life, we often find ourselves at crossroads, faced with choices and decisions that shape our path. Whether big or small, these choices hold immense power in determining the course of our lives. Taking responsibility for our actions is an essential aspect of personal accountability, and it is through owning our choices and decisions that we truly take control of our lives.

Every one of us has the power to make choices, and it is crucial to recognize that with this power comes responsibility. When we own our choices, we acknowledge that we are in control of our lives and that our actions have consequences. By taking responsibility for our decisions, we free ourselves from the victim mentality and empower ourselves to create the life we desire.

Owning our choices and decisions requires self-awareness and a commitment to personal growth. It means recognizing that we have the power to choose our responses to any given situation, even when circumstances seem unfavorable. It is easy to blame external factors for our failures or shortcomings, but true personal accountability lies in acknowledging that we have the ability to shape our own destiny.

When we take ownership of our choices, we become more mindful in our decision-making process. We understand that every choice we make has the potential to bring us closer to our goals or lead us astray. By considering the long-term implications of our decisions, we can align our choices with our values and aspirations. This mindfulness allows us to make decisions that are in line with our authentic selves, leading to a more fulfilling and purpose-driven life.

Moreover, owning our choices and decisions fosters personal growth and development. When we accept responsibility for our actions, we open ourselves up to learning from our mistakes and failures. Rather than dwelling on past missteps, we can use them as stepping stones towards self-improvement. Embracing the lessons learned from our choices empowers us to make better decisions in the future, leading to personal and professional growth.

In conclusion, owning our choices and decisions is a fundamental aspect of personal accountability. By taking responsibility for our actions, we reclaim our power and become active participants in shaping our lives. It is through this ownership that we cultivate self-awareness, make mindful decisions, and foster personal growth. So, let us embrace the power of owning our choices and decisions and take control of our lives.

Overcoming the Fear of Failure and Success

Fear can be a powerful force that holds us back from reaching our full potential. Whether it is fear of failure or fear of success, these emotions can prevent us from taking risks and pursuing our dreams. In the subchapter "Overcoming the Fear of Failure and Success" from the book "The Power of Personal Accountability: Taking Control of Your Life," we will explore strategies to help you overcome these fears and take responsibility for your actions.

Fear of failure is something that many people experience throughout their lives. It is a fear of not living up to our own expectations or the expectations of others. This fear can be paralyzing, causing us to avoid taking risks and staying within our comfort zone. However, it is important to remember that failure is a part of life and a stepping stone towards success. By reframing failure as an opportunity to learn and grow, we can overcome this fear and embrace new challenges.

On the other hand, fear of success can also be a significant barrier to personal growth. It is a fear of the unknown and the responsibilities that come with success. We may worry about how our lives will change, or fear that we will be unable to maintain our success in the long run. However, by shifting our mindset and focusing on the positive aspects of success, we can overcome this fear and fully embrace our potential.

Taking responsibility for our actions is crucial in overcoming these fears. By recognizing that we have control over our own lives and the choices we make, we can empower ourselves to overcome obstacles and achieve our goals. It is important to understand that failure and success are not solely determined by external factors but are influenced by our own actions and decisions.

In order to overcome the fear of failure and success, it is essential to develop a growth mindset. This means embracing challenges, viewing failure as an opportunity to learn, and persisting in the face of setbacks. Additionally, setting realistic goals, creating a support system, and practicing self-compassion are invaluable strategies for overcoming these fears.

Remember, overcoming the fear of failure and success is a journey that requires self-reflection, perseverance, and a willingness to step outside of your comfort zone. By taking responsibility for your actions and embracing the unknown, you can unlock your true potential and take control of your life. So, let go of your fears, believe in yourself, and start living a life of personal accountability.

Chapter 3: Taking Responsibility for Your Actions

Acknowledging Your Mistakes

In life, we all make mistakes. It's a fact of being human. However, what sets us apart is how we choose to respond to those mistakes. Taking responsibility for our actions is a crucial aspect of personal accountability. It allows us to grow, learn, and become better versions of ourselves.

Acknowledging your mistakes is the first step towards personal growth and accountability. It requires a certain level of self-awareness and humility. By recognizing when we have made a mistake, we can actively take steps towards rectifying the situation and preventing similar errors in the future.

One of the key reasons why acknowledging mistakes is so important is that it promotes a healthy sense of self-reflection. When we take responsibility for our actions, we are forced to examine our behaviors and decisions. This self-reflection allows us to identify patterns, weaknesses, and areas for improvement. By acknowledging our mistakes, we can learn from them and make better choices moving forward.

Furthermore, taking responsibility for our actions is not only important for our personal growth but also for our relationships with others. When we admit our mistakes, it shows integrity and sincerity. It demonstrates that we value honesty and are willing to make amends. This can help repair damaged relationships and build trust with those around us.

It's important to remember that acknowledging our mistakes does not make us weak or inadequate. On the contrary, it takes strength and courage to admit when we have done wrong. It shows that we are willing to face the consequences of our actions and strive for improvement.

In order to effectively acknowledge our mistakes, it is necessary to adopt a growth mindset. Instead of viewing failures as final, we should see them as opportunities for growth and learning. By embracing this mindset, we can approach our mistakes with curiosity and a desire to understand how we can do better next time.

In conclusion, acknowledging our mistakes is an essential part of personal accountability. It allows us to grow, learn, and take control of our lives. By taking responsibility for our actions, we promote self-reflection, build stronger relationships, and develop a growth mindset. So, let us embrace our mistakes as stepping stones towards personal growth and success.

Learning from Failures and Moving Forward

Failure is an inevitable part of life. Whether we like it or not, we are bound to face setbacks and disappointments along our journey. However, what sets successful individuals apart from others is their ability to learn from these failures and use them as stepping stones towards personal growth and achievement. In this subchapter, we will explore the importance of taking responsibility for our actions, embracing failure as a valuable learning experience, and moving forward with resilience and determination.

Taking responsibility for our actions is the cornerstone of personal accountability. It means acknowledging that our choices and decisions have consequences, both positive and negative. By accepting responsibility, we empower ourselves to make better choices in the future and take control of our lives. Avoiding blame or making excuses only hinders our personal growth and prevents us from learning valuable lessons.

When we encounter failure, it is crucial to shift our perspective and view it as an opportunity for growth. Failure should not be seen as a reflection of our worth or abilities, but rather as a chance to learn, adapt, and improve. By analyzing our failures objectively, we can identify the mistakes we made and develop strategies to avoid repeating them. Failure becomes a catalyst for progress and a powerful motivator to strive for success.

Moving forward from failure requires resilience and determination. It is natural to feel discouraged and demotivated after experiencing setbacks, but it is essential to bounce back and keep moving forward.

Cultivating a positive mindset and focusing on the lessons learned rather than dwelling on the past is vital for personal development. We must embrace failure as an integral part of the learning process and use it to fuel our determination to succeed.

In conclusion, taking responsibility for our actions and learning from failures are crucial aspects of personal accountability. By accepting responsibility, we empower ourselves to make better choices and take control of our lives. Failure should be viewed as an opportunity for growth and a valuable learning experience. Moving forward from failure requires resilience and determination, but by embracing failure and using it as a stepping stone towards success, we can achieve personal growth and reach our full potential. Remember, every failure brings us one step closer to success.

Accepting Consequences and Making Amends

Accepting Consequences and Making Amends: Taking Responsibility for Your Actions

In life, we all make mistakes. It's a part of being human. However, what truly separates responsible individuals from the rest is their ability to accept the consequences of their actions and make amends. This subchapter explores the importance of taking personal accountability and provides practical strategies for embracing the power of accepting consequences.

Accepting consequences requires a shift in mindset. Instead of blaming others or making excuses, it involves acknowledging our role in the situation and recognizing the impact of our actions. It's about realizing that we have the power to shape our lives through our choices. By accepting consequences, we empower ourselves to learn from our mistakes and grow as individuals.

Making amends is an essential part of accepting consequences. It involves taking steps to rectify any harm caused by our actions. This could be through apologies, restitution, or even community service. Making amends demonstrates that we are committed to making things right and rebuilding trust. It shows that we are willing to go beyond mere words and take action to repair the damage caused.

Taking responsibility for our actions is vital because it leads to personal growth and development. When we accept consequences, we learn valuable lessons that help us avoid repeating the same mistakes in the future. It allows us to cultivate empathy and understanding towards others, as we realize the impact our actions can have on their lives. By taking responsibility, we become more self-aware and gain a deeper understanding of our values and principles.

To embrace personal accountability, it is crucial to develop self-reflection skills. This involves taking the time to evaluate our actions, motivations, and the underlying beliefs that led to our choices. By understanding the root causes, we can address them and make positive changes in our lives. Self-reflection also allows us to recognize patterns and triggers that may lead to irresponsible behavior, enabling us to proactively avoid them.

In conclusion, accepting consequences and making amends is an essential aspect of personal accountability. It requires us to shift our mindset, take responsibility for our actions, and actively work towards rectifying any harm caused. By embracing this power, we can grow as individuals, gain self-awareness, and foster meaningful relationships with others. Remember, it's never too late to make amends and take control of your lifc.

Chapter 4: Building Personal Accountability in Relationships

Taking Responsibility for Your Role in Relationships

In this subchapter, we will delve into the crucial concept of taking responsibility for your role in relationships. Relationships are an integral part of our lives, whether they be with family, friends, romantic partners, or colleagues. However, all too often, we find ourselves blaming others or external circumstances for the problems we face in these relationships. The truth is, we have the power to transform our relationships by taking personal accountability for our actions and roles within them.

One of the key aspects of taking responsibility for your role in relationships is recognizing that you are not solely a victim or a passive observer. You have the ability to impact the dynamics and outcomes of your relationships through your thoughts, words, and actions. By understanding this, you can begin to take ownership of your behavior and make conscious choices that contribute positively to your relationships.

It is essential to reflect on your actions and their consequences on your relationships. Often, we engage in behaviors that may inadvertently harm the people we care about. By taking responsibility for these actions, we can acknowledge the impact they have had and work towards making amends. This process requires humility and self-awareness, but it is a crucial step towards building healthier and more fulfilling relationships.

Another aspect of taking responsibility for your role in relationships is actively seeking to understand the perspectives and needs of others. This requires open communication and empathy. By truly listening and considering the feelings and experiences of those around us, we can foster stronger connections and develop a deeper understanding of each other's needs.

Furthermore, taking responsibility for your role in relationships involves setting healthy boundaries. It is important to establish clear expectations and communicate them effectively to avoid misunderstandings and conflicts. By doing so, you can prevent resentment from building up and ensure that both parties feel respected and valued.

Ultimately, taking responsibility for your role in relationships empowers you to be an active participant in shaping the dynamics and outcomes. By recognizing your ability to make positive changes, you can build stronger, more fulfilling relationships with those around you.

In conclusion, taking responsibility for your role in relationships is a vital aspect of personal accountability. By acknowledging your impact, reflecting on your actions, seeking understanding, and setting boundaries, you can transform your relationships and create a more harmonious and fulfilling life. Remember, you have the power to take control and make a positive difference in your relationships, no matter who you are or what your circumstances may be.

Communicating Effectively and Resolving Conflicts

In our journey towards personal accountability, one crucial aspect we must master is effective communication and conflict resolution. These skills not only allow us to express ourselves clearly but also foster healthy relationships and create a positive impact on those around us. By taking responsibility for our actions in these areas, we can enhance our personal growth and foster a more harmonious environment.

Effective communication begins with active listening. By genuinely hearing and understanding others, we can respond thoughtfully and empathetically. It is important to be present in conversations, eliminating distractions and giving our undivided attention. This demonstrates respect and builds trust, enabling us to connect on a deeper level. Furthermore, using open-ended questions and paraphrasing what we hear can help clarify any misunderstandings and ensure accurate comprehension.

Another vital aspect of effective communication is expressing our thoughts and feelings clearly. We must take responsibility for articulating our needs, boundaries, and expectations. By using "I" statements instead of accusatory language, we can avoid triggering defensiveness and encourage open dialogue. Additionally, practicing assertiveness allows us to stand up for ourselves while still considering the needs of others.

Conflicts are an inevitable part of life, and being accountable means addressing them in a constructive manner. Conflict resolution involves actively seeking solutions that meet the needs of all parties involved. It starts with acknowledging our own role in the conflict and taking responsibility for our actions. By avoiding blame and instead focusing on finding common ground, we can promote understanding and cooperation.

One powerful tool for resolving conflicts is active problem-solving. This method involves identifying the root cause of the conflict, brainstorming possible solutions, and evaluating the pros and cons of each suggestion. By involving all parties in this process, we can foster collaboration and ensure that everyone feels heard and valued.

Effective communication and conflict resolution skills are invaluable in all aspects of life, whether at work, in relationships, or within communities. By taking responsibility for our actions in these areas, we create a culture of accountability and contribute to a more positive and fulfilling environment for everyone.

Remember, effective communication is a lifelong skill that requires practice and continuous improvement. By constantly refining our ability to express ourselves and resolve conflicts, we empower ourselves to take control of our lives and create meaningful connections with those around us. Let us embrace the power of personal accountability and strive for effective communication and conflict resolution in all aspects of our lives.

Holding Yourself Accountable in Collaborative Efforts

Collaboration is a powerful tool that can lead to amazing results when individuals come together to work towards a common goal. Whether it's a team project at work, a community initiative, or a personal relationship, collaborative efforts can be highly effective. However, in order for collaboration to be successful, it is crucial for each individual involved to take responsibility for their actions and hold themselves accountable.

Taking responsibility for your actions is an essential aspect of personal accountability. It means owning up to your mistakes, acknowledging your contributions, and being proactive in finding solutions. When working collaboratively, it is vital to recognize the impact of your actions on the overall project or relationship. By holding yourself accountable, you not only ensure that you are meeting your commitments, but you also inspire others to do the same.

One way to hold yourself accountable in collaborative efforts is by setting clear goals and expectations. Clearly defining the desired outcomes and the roles and responsibilities of each team member helps to establish a sense of ownership. By understanding what is expected of you, you can take the necessary actions to fulfill your obligations. Regularly reviewing these goals and expectations as a team can also help to identify any deviations or areas for improvement.

Another crucial aspect of personal accountability in collaboration is effective communication. Open and honest communication is key to building trust and maintaining accountability within a team. It is important to express your thoughts, ideas, and concerns, while also actively listening to others. By fostering a culture of open communication, team members can hold each other accountable by providing constructive feedback, addressing any issues, and celebrating achievements.

Accountability also requires self-reflection and self-awareness. It is important to regularly assess your own performance, identify areas for growth, and make necessary adjustments. This involves being honest with yourself about your strengths and weaknesses and taking proactive steps towards self-improvement. By continuously learning and growing, you not only enhance your own accountability but also contribute to the overall success of the collaborative effort.

In conclusion, holding yourself accountable in collaborative efforts is crucial for achieving successful outcomes. By taking responsibility for your actions, setting clear goals, communicating effectively, and engaging in self-reflection, you can contribute to a culture of personal accountability within a team or relationship. Remember, personal accountability is not just about meeting your own commitments; it is about inspiring others to do the same and creating an environment where everyone can thrive.

Chapter 5: Personal Accountability in the Workplace

Understanding Your Role and Responsibilities

Taking responsibility for your actions is a fundamental aspect of personal accountability. In today's fast-paced and interconnected world, it is more important than ever to understand your role and responsibilities in order to take control of your life. This subchapter aims to provide you with a deeper understanding of your role and responsibilities, empowering you to become the best version of yourself.

First and foremost, it is crucial to recognize that you are the captain of your own ship. You have the power to steer the course of your life and make the necessary decisions to shape your future. By taking responsibility for your actions, you acknowledge that the outcomes of your choices lie in your hands. This mindset allows you to embrace the power of personal accountability, leading to growth and success in all aspects of your life.

Understanding your role involves recognizing that you are not alone in this journey. You are part of a larger community, whether it be your family, friends, colleagues, or society as a whole. Your actions have an impact on those around you, and it is your responsibility to ensure that this impact is positive. By taking ownership of your actions, you become a role model and inspire others to do the same.

Moreover, understanding your responsibilities goes beyond your immediate circle. It extends to the world we live in, including our environment, the economy, and social issues. Each one of us has a duty to contribute to the betterment of society. This can be achieved through acts of kindness, volunteering, or even making conscious choices that minimize our ecological footprint. By recognizing and fulfilling these responsibilities, you become an active participant in creating a better world for future generations.

Taking responsibility for your actions is not always an easy task. It requires self-reflection, honesty, and the willingness to learn from your mistakes. However, the rewards are immeasurable. By embracing personal accountability, you gain a sense of empowerment, resilience, and purpose. You become the driver of your own destiny, capable of achieving your goals and dreams.

In conclusion, understanding your role and responsibilities is essential for personal growth and success. By taking ownership of your actions, you become the architect of your life, positively impacting those around you and contributing to the betterment of society. Embrace personal accountability, and unlock the power to take control of your life.

Setting Clear Goals and Expectations

In the journey towards personal accountability, one of the most crucial steps is setting clear goals and expectations for oneself. By doing so, we take control of our lives, shaping our future according to our desires and aspirations. This subchapter aims to guide every individual, regardless of their background or circumstances, in taking responsibility for their actions through the process of goal-setting.

To begin with, it is essential to understand the power of defining clear goals. Without a clear direction, we may find ourselves lost, lacking motivation, and unable to take ownership of our lives. By setting specific, measurable, achievable, relevant, and time-bound (SMART) goals, we create a roadmap that allows us to track our progress and take pride in our accomplishments. These goals should be aligned with our values and passions, ensuring that we stay committed and driven towards success.

Furthermore, it is important to manage our expectations realistically. Often, individuals fall into the trap of setting unrealistic expectations, leading to frustration and a sense of failure. By setting achievable goals, we set ourselves up for success, building confidence and a sense of personal accountability along the way. It is crucial to remember that progress takes time, and setbacks are a natural part of the journey. Embracing a growth mindset and learning from failures will enable us to stay focused, adapt, and persevere.

Additionally, effective communication plays a vital role in setting clear goals and expectations. It is essential to communicate our intentions and aspirations to those around us, whether it be our family, friends, or colleagues. By doing so, we create a support system that encourages us to stay accountable and provides guidance during challenging times. Moreover, effective communication helps avoid misunderstandings and ensures that others understand our objectives, making collaboration and cooperation easier.

In conclusion, taking personal accountability requires setting clear goals and expectations. By defining our aspirations, managing our expectations, and effectively communicating our intentions, we empower ourselves to take control of our lives. This subchapter is a call to action for every individual, regardless of their background or circumstances, to embrace the power of goal-setting and take responsibility for their actions. Remember, the journey towards personal accountability begins with clarity and commitment to the goals we set for ourselves.

Taking Initiative and Demonstrating Accountability

In our journey through life, we often find ourselves faced with situations where we must take responsibility for our actions. It is in these moments that our true character is revealed, as we are given the opportunity to demonstrate our accountability. This subchapter explores the importance of taking initiative and the power of personal accountability in every aspect of our lives.

Taking responsibility for our actions is not always an easy task. It requires a level of self-awareness and the willingness to face the consequences of our decisions. However, it is through this process that we empower ourselves to make positive changes and take control of our lives.

One key aspect of taking initiative is recognizing that we have the power to influence outcomes. Instead of simply accepting the circumstances that come our way, we can actively seek opportunities to make a difference. By taking the initiative, we become proactive problem solvers and agents of change.

Accountability goes hand in hand with taking initiative. It is about owning up to our mistakes, admitting when we are wrong, and taking the necessary steps to rectify the situation. When we hold ourselves accountable, we not only earn the respect of others but also gain a sense of personal satisfaction and growth.

Taking responsibility for our actions extends beyond the professional realm; it permeates into all aspects of our lives. Whether it is in our relationships, health, or personal goals, being accountable allows us to take charge and create the life we desire. It is about recognizing that we have the power to shape our own destiny.

In this subchapter, we will explore practical strategies for taking initiative and demonstrating accountability. From setting clear goals and creating action plans to embracing challenges and learning from failures, we will delve into the tools and mindset needed to embrace personal accountability.

By embracing the power of personal accountability, we can transform our lives and the lives of those around us. It is through taking initiative and demonstrating accountability that we become the best version of ourselves. So, whether you are a student, a professional, or simply someone seeking personal growth, this subchapter will provide you with the guidance and inspiration to take control of your life and embrace the power of personal accountability.

Chapter 6: Overcoming Procrastination and Building Discipline

Identifying the Root Causes of Procrastination

Procrastination is a common struggle that affects people from all walks of life. Whether it's putting off important tasks, delaying decision-making, or avoiding responsibilities, we have all experienced the detrimental effects of procrastination at some point. In this subchapter, we will delve into the root causes of procrastination and explore how taking personal accountability can help overcome this self-defeating behavior.

One of the primary reasons behind procrastination is fear. Fear of failure, fear of success, fear of judgment – these insecurities often paralyze us and prevent us from taking action. By recognizing and acknowledging these fears, we can begin to understand how they contribute to our tendency to procrastinate. Taking responsibility for our actions involves confronting these fears head-on and challenging the negative thoughts that hold us back.

Another root cause of procrastination is a lack of clarity and purpose. When we are unsure about our goals or lack a clear vision for our future, it becomes easy to put off tasks that seem overwhelming or unrelated to our aspirations. By taking personal accountability, we can take the time to reflect on our values, set meaningful goals, and prioritize our actions accordingly. This clarity not only provides us with a sense of purpose but also helps us overcome the urge to procrastinate.

Furthermore, perfectionism often fuels procrastination. The fear of not being able to meet impossibly high standards can lead to avoidance and delay. By embracing personal accountability, we can shift our focus from seeking perfection to valuing progress. Recognizing that taking imperfect action is better than taking no action at all empowers us to overcome the paralyzing effects of perfectionism.

Lastly, our mindset and habits play a significant role in perpetuating procrastination. Negative thought patterns, such as self-doubt or a lack of confidence, can hinder our ability to take action. By cultivating a growth mindset and developing positive habits, we can build resilience and motivation to tackle tasks head-on. Personal accountability involves consciously choosing to replace self-defeating thoughts and behaviors with empowering ones.

In conclusion, identifying the root causes of procrastination is crucial for taking personal accountability and overcoming this self-sabotaging behavior. By addressing fear, gaining clarity, letting go of perfectionism, and cultivating a positive mindset, we can break free from the cycle of procrastination and take control of our lives. Embracing personal accountability empowers us to become more productive, achieve our goals, and lead a fulfilling and purposeful life.

Strategies for Overcoming Procrastination

Procrastination is a common struggle that many people face in their daily lives. It is the act of delaying or postponing tasks, often resulting in increased stress and decreased productivity. However, by implementing effective strategies, anyone can overcome procrastination and take control of their life. In this subchapter, we will explore some powerful techniques that will help you tackle this issue head-on and develop a sense of personal accountability.

One of the most effective strategies for overcoming procrastination is setting clear and realistic goals. By defining your objectives and breaking them down into smaller, manageable tasks, you can create a clear roadmap for yourself. Additionally, setting deadlines for each task will help you stay focused and motivated. Remember to prioritize your tasks based on their importance and urgency, allowing you to allocate your time and energy efficiently.

Another strategy for overcoming procrastination is to eliminate distractions. In today's digital age, it is easy to get sidetracked by social media, emails, or other non-essential activities. To combat this, consider creating a designated workspace free from distractions. Turn off notifications on your phone or computer and establish specific times for checking emails or engaging in social media. By minimizing distractions, you can optimize your productivity and reduce the temptation to procrastinate.

Furthermore, adopting a positive mindset is crucial when combating procrastination. Negative thoughts and self-doubt can often lead to procrastination. Instead, focus on the benefits and rewards that come from completing tasks promptly. Celebrate small victories along the way, as this will reinforce positive habits and motivate you to continue being proactive.

Accountability partners can also be a valuable tool in overcoming procrastination. Share your goals and progress with someone you trust, such as a friend, family member, or mentor. They can provide guidance, encouragement, and hold you accountable for your actions. Regular check-ins and open discussions will help you stay on track and maintain your commitment to personal accountability.

In conclusion, overcoming procrastination requires a combination of effective strategies and a mindset shift. By setting clear goals, eliminating distractions, adopting a positive mindset, and seeking accountability, you can conquer procrastination and take control of your life. Remember, personal accountability is the key to success, and by implementing these strategies, you are well on your way to achieving your goals and living a more fulfilling and productive life.

Cultivating Discipline and Consistency

Taking responsibility for your actions is a fundamental aspect of personal accountability. It is about acknowledging that you are in control of your own life and the choices you make. In order to truly take control of your life, you must cultivate discipline and consistency.

Discipline is the key to achieving your goals and living a fulfilling life. It is the ability to stay focused, committed, and motivated even when faced with challenges and obstacles. When you cultivate discipline, you develop the mental strength to resist distractions and make choices that align with your values and long-term objectives.

Consistency is equally important in the journey towards personal accountability. It is the practice of consistently showing up and putting in the effort required to achieve your desired outcomes. Consistency builds trust, not only with others but also with yourself. When you consistently follow through on your commitments and take responsibility for your actions, you become someone that others can rely on and trust.

To cultivate discipline and consistency, it is important to set clear and specific goals. Knowing what you want to achieve and why it is important to you will help you stay motivated and focused. Break down your goals into smaller, manageable tasks and create a schedule or routine to ensure that you consistently work towards them.

In addition, it is important to develop self-awareness. Understand your strengths and weaknesses, and be honest with yourself about areas that may require more discipline or consistency. Recognize patterns or habits that may hinder your progress and actively work towards replacing them with more positive and productive behaviors.

Another valuable strategy is to surround yourself with like-minded individuals who share your commitment to personal accountability. Seek out mentors or accountability partners who can provide guidance and support along your journey. Being part of a community that values discipline and consistency can help you stay motivated and accountable.

Remember, personal accountability is a lifelong practice. It requires consistent effort and a commitment to growth and self-improvement. By cultivating discipline and consistency, you will not only take control of your life but also inspire and empower others to do the same.

Chapter 7: Cultivating a Growth Mindset

Embracing Challenges and Seeing Opportunities

In the journey of life, challenges and opportunities are inevitable. They come in various forms and sizes, testing our resilience and determination. However, it is how we respond to these challenges and perceive the opportunities that truly shape our lives. In this subchapter, we will delve into the power of taking responsibility for our actions and how it can help us embrace challenges and see opportunities with a fresh perspective.

Taking responsibility for our actions is a fundamental aspect of personal accountability. It is about acknowledging that we have the power to control our lives and the choices we make. When we fully grasp this concept, we realize that challenges are not roadblocks but stepping stones towards growth and success.

Instead of shying away from challenges, we should embrace them as opportunities for personal development. Challenges force us to step out of our comfort zones, learn new skills, and discover our strengths. They push us to overcome obstacles and build resilience. By taking responsibility for our actions, we can transform challenges into catalysts for growth, enabling us to reach our full potential.

Moreover, embracing challenges allows us to see opportunities that may have otherwise gone unnoticed. When we have a positive mindset and take ownership of our actions, we become more open to new possibilities. We start to see opportunities where others see obstacles.

By reframing challenges as opportunities, we can unlock our creative potential and find innovative solutions.

Taking responsibility for our actions also means accepting the consequences of our choices. It is about understanding that our decisions have an impact not only on ourselves but also on those around us. By being accountable, we can cultivate trust and respect in our relationships, both personally and professionally.

In conclusion, embracing challenges and seeing opportunities requires a mindset shift towards personal accountability. By taking responsibility for our actions, we can transform challenges into growth opportunities and uncover hidden possibilities. It is through this mindset that we can truly take control of our lives and reach our fullest potential. So, let us embrace challenges, take ownership of our actions, and open our minds to the endless possibilities that lie ahead.

Viewing Setbacks as Learning Experiences

In our journey through life, setbacks are inevitable. They can come in various forms - a failed relationship, a lost opportunity, a business venture gone wrong, or a personal mistake. It is easy to feel discouraged and disheartened when faced with setbacks, but it is essential to remember that setbacks can also be valuable learning experiences. By viewing setbacks as opportunities for growth and learning, we can take control of our lives and develop a greater sense of personal accountability.

Taking responsibility for our actions is a fundamental aspect of personal accountability. When we encounter setbacks, it is tempting to blame external factors or other people for our failures. However, true personal accountability requires us to look within ourselves and reflect on our own contributions to the setback. By taking responsibility for our actions, we empower ourselves to learn from our mistakes and make positive changes in our lives.

One way to view setbacks as learning experiences is to adopt a growth mindset. Rather than seeing setbacks as permanent failures, we can recognize them as temporary obstacles on the path to success. With a growth mindset, we understand that setbacks provide opportunities for self-improvement and personal development. We can approach setbacks with curiosity and a desire to learn, knowing that they will ultimately make us stronger and more resilient individuals.

Another important aspect of viewing setbacks as learning experiences is the ability to extract lessons from them. Setbacks often reveal areas where we need to improve or develop new skills. By reflecting on the reasons behind our setbacks, we can identify areas for growth and take proactive steps to address them. This might involve seeking additional training, reaching out for mentorship, or adjusting our approach to future endeavors.

Furthermore, setbacks can teach us valuable life lessons about resilience, perseverance, and adaptability. They remind us that success is not always a linear path but rather a series of ups and downs. By embracing setbacks as part of our personal growth journey, we develop the strength and determination to overcome obstacles and achieve our goals.

In conclusion, setbacks should not be viewed as failures but rather as learning experiences. Taking responsibility for our actions and adopting a growth mindset allows us to extract valuable lessons from setbacks and use them as opportunities for personal growth. By viewing setbacks as learning experiences, we can develop a greater sense of personal accountability and take control of our lives. So, the next time you face a setback, remember that it is just another chance to learn, grow, and become a better version of yourself.

Seeking Continuous Improvement and Personal Growth

In today's fast-paced world, it is crucial for every individual to take responsibility for their actions and strive for continuous improvement and personal growth. In the book "The Power of Personal Accountability: Taking Control of Your Life," we delve into the significance of this mindset and how it can transform your life for the better.

Taking responsibility for your actions is the foundation of personal accountability. It means acknowledging that you are in control of your choices, behaviors, and outcomes. This mindset empowers you to make conscious decisions that align with your values and goals. When you accept responsibility, you no longer blame external factors for your circumstances but instead focus on finding solutions and taking proactive steps towards improvement.

Continuous improvement is a lifelong process of honing your skills, knowledge, and mindset. It is about constantly seeking opportunities to learn, grow, and evolve. By embracing this mindset, you open yourself up to new experiences, challenges, and perspectives. It allows you to push beyond your comfort zone, embrace change, and adapt to new situations. Continuous improvement not only propels your personal growth but also ensures that you stay relevant and competitive in today's dynamic world.

Personal growth goes hand in hand with continuous improvement. It involves developing your character, values, and emotional intelligence. Personal growth is not limited to acquiring new skills but also encompasses cultivating self-awareness, empathy, resilience, and a growth mindset. It is about becoming the best version of yourself and realizing your full potential. Personal growth enhances your relationships, career prospects, and overall well-being.

To embark on the journey of seeking continuous improvement and personal growth, it is essential to adopt certain strategies. First and foremost, set clear and challenging goals that align with your values. Break these goals down into smaller, manageable tasks to stay motivated and track your progress. Embrace a growth mindset, viewing challenges as opportunities for learning and growth. Surround yourself with positive and supportive individuals who inspire and motivate you. Seek feedback and be open to constructive criticism, as it allows for self-reflection and improvement. Additionally, embrace lifelong learning by reading, attending seminars, or taking up new hobbies.

In conclusion, seeking continuous improvement and personal growth is a lifelong commitment that requires taking responsibility for your actions and investing in self-development. By embracing this mindset, you can unlock your true potential, achieve success in various aspects of life, and lead a fulfilling and purposeful existence. So, take charge of your life, embrace personal accountability, and start your journey towards continuous improvement and personal growth today!

Chapter 8: Accountability in Health and Wellness

Taking Responsibility for Your Physical Health

In today's fast-paced world, it is easy to neglect our physical health. We often find ourselves caught up in the demands of work, family, and other responsibilities, leaving little time for self-care. However, taking responsibility for our physical health is crucial for leading a fulfilling and productive life. It is an essential aspect of personal accountability, as it directly affects our overall well-being and ability to take control of our lives.

First and foremost, taking responsibility for your physical health means acknowledging that you have the power to make choices that will positively impact your well-being. It means understanding that your actions, or lack thereof, have consequences. By taking ownership of your physical health, you are taking a proactive stance towards improving and maintaining your body's vitality.

One of the key ways to take responsibility for your physical health is through regular exercise. Engaging in physical activity not only helps to maintain a healthy weight but also boosts energy levels, improves mood, and reduces the risk of various health conditions. Whether it's going for a jog, practicing yoga, or joining a gym, finding an exercise routine that suits your lifestyle and preferences is vital.

Another crucial aspect of taking responsibility for your physical health is adopting a balanced and nutritious diet. Nourishing your body with wholesome foods, rich in vitamins, minerals, and antioxidants, provides the fuel it needs to function optimally. Avoiding excessive consumption of processed foods, sugary drinks, and unhealthy snacks is essential for maintaining a healthy weight and preventing chronic diseases.

Additionally, taking responsibility for your physical health involves prioritizing rest and relaxation. Adequate sleep is crucial for rejuvenating the body and mind, as it supports cognitive function, immune health, and emotional well-being. Establishing a consistent sleep schedule and creating a relaxing bedtime routine can significantly contribute to overall physical health.

Lastly, regular check-ups with healthcare professionals are essential for monitoring and maintaining your physical health. By scheduling regular appointments with your doctor, dentist, and other specialists, you can detect and address any potential health issues early on, ensuring prompt intervention and treatment.

Taking responsibility for your physical health is an ongoing journey. It requires commitment, discipline, and a willingness to prioritize self-care. However, the rewards are immeasurable. By making conscious choices to prioritize exercise, nutrition, rest, and regular check-ups, you are empowering yourself to take control of your physical well-being and live a vibrant and fulfilling life.

Remember, you are the captain of your ship, and only by embracing personal accountability for your physical health can you navigate the seas of life with strength and vitality.

Nurturing Your Mental and Emotional Well-being

In today's fast-paced and demanding world, it is vital to prioritize our mental and emotional well-being. Taking responsibility for our actions is not just about being accountable for the outcomes; it also includes nurturing our mental and emotional health. In this subchapter, we will explore the significance of maintaining a healthy mindset and emotional balance and provide practical strategies to achieve this.

Our mental and emotional well-being directly influences our overall quality of life. When we neglect our mental and emotional health, we become more susceptible to stress, anxiety, and burnout. Therefore, it is essential to prioritize self-care and invest time and effort into nurturing our well-being.

One of the key aspects of nurturing our mental and emotional well-being is practicing self-awareness. This involves recognizing and acknowledging our emotions, thoughts, and behaviors without judgment. By becoming more self-aware, we can identify any negative patterns or triggers that may be hindering our well-being. This awareness empowers us to make conscious choices and take responsibility for our actions.

Another vital aspect of nurturing our mental and emotional well-being is practicing self-compassion. It is crucial to treat ourselves with kindness and understanding, especially during challenging times. Self-compassion involves acknowledging our imperfections and embracing them as part of being human. By cultivating self-compassion, we develop resilience and the ability to bounce back from setbacks.

Furthermore, nurturing our mental and emotional well-being requires us to establish healthy boundaries. This means setting limits on the demands and expectations we place on ourselves and others. By setting boundaries, we protect our mental and emotional energy, allowing us to focus on what truly matters and avoid unnecessary stress.

Additionally, incorporating mindfulness practices into our daily routines can greatly benefit our mental and emotional well-being. Mindfulness involves being fully present in the moment, non-judgmentally observing our thoughts and feelings. By practicing mindfulness, we can reduce stress, enhance self-awareness, and cultivate a sense of calm and clarity.

In conclusion, nurturing our mental and emotional well-being is a crucial part of taking responsibility for our actions. By prioritizing self-care, practicing self-awareness, self-compassion, setting healthy boundaries, and incorporating mindfulness practices into our lives, we can elevate our overall well-being. Remember, taking care of ourselves is not a luxury but a necessity for leading a fulfilling and accountable life.

Creating Healthy Habits and Routines

Taking responsibility for your actions is a fundamental aspect of personal accountability. It allows you to recognize that your choices and behaviors have consequences, and empowers you to take control of your life. One way to enhance personal accountability is by creating healthy habits and routines. These habits can help you become more disciplined, focused, and ultimately lead to a more fulfilling and successful life.

Developing healthy habits starts with setting clear goals. Ask yourself what you want to achieve in different areas of your life – be it in your career, relationships, health, or personal growth. Once you have identified your goals, break them down into smaller, achievable tasks. This will make it easier to create a routine that supports your aspirations.

Consistency is key when it comes to forming healthy habits. Make a commitment to yourself to engage in these habits on a regular basis. Whether it's exercising for 30 minutes every morning, dedicating time to read and learn every day, or practicing self-reflection and gratitude before bed, find a routine that works for you and stick to it. Remember, it takes time for habits to become ingrained, so be patient with yourself.

To stay motivated and accountable, consider finding an accountability partner or joining a support group. Having someone who shares your goals and can hold you accountable can greatly increase your chances of success. Additionally, tracking your progress can provide a visual reminder of how far you have come and help you stay on track.

Creating healthy habits and routines also involves eliminating negative influences from your life. Identify any habits or behaviors that are hindering your progress and make a conscious effort to replace them with positive alternatives. Surround yourself with people who motivate and inspire you, and seek out environments that support your goals.

Lastly, be kind and forgiving to yourself. Remember that forming healthy habits is a journey, and setbacks are a natural part of the process. Be patient, learn from your mistakes, and keep pushing forward. By creating healthy habits and routines, you are taking control of your life and paving the way for personal accountability and success.

Chapter 9: Empowering Yourself Through Personal Accountability

Setting Boundaries and Prioritizing Self-Care

In today's fast-paced and demanding world, taking responsibility for our actions is crucial. It is the foundation upon which personal accountability is built, enabling us to take control of our lives. However, amidst the chaos and demands of daily life, we often neglect the most important person in the equation – ourselves. This subchapter aims to shed light on the significance of setting boundaries and prioritizing self-care in order to truly embrace personal accountability.

Setting boundaries is essential for maintaining a healthy balance in all aspects of life. Whether it's in our professional or personal relationships, setting clear limits helps prevent others from infringing upon our time, energy, and emotional well-being. By clearly defining what is acceptable and what is not, we establish a standard of respect and create space for personal growth. Setting boundaries allows us to focus on our own needs and desires, ultimately leading to a more fulfilling and purposeful life.

Prioritizing self-care is often misconstrued as selfishness. However, self-care is not a luxury; it is a necessity. It involves taking intentional steps to nurture and nourish ourselves physically, emotionally, and mentally. Engaging in activities that bring us joy, practicing self-compassion, and taking time for rest and relaxation are all vital components of self-care. By prioritizing self-care, we replenish our energy, reduce stress, and enhance our overall well-being. It becomes easier to take responsibility for our actions when we are in a healthy state of mind and body.

In order to truly embrace personal accountability, we must recognize that taking care of ourselves is not an indulgence, but a responsibility. We cannot pour from an empty cup. By setting boundaries and making self-care a priority, we empower ourselves to be more present, engaged, and accountable in all areas of our lives.

It is important to remember that personal accountability is not about perfection or always getting it right. It is about taking ownership of our choices, actions, and outcomes. It is about learning from our mistakes and making conscious decisions that align with our values and goals. By setting boundaries and prioritizing self-care, we create the necessary foundation for personal accountability to thrive.

In conclusion, setting boundaries and prioritizing self-care are essential elements of personal accountability. They enable us to take control of our lives, make intentional choices, and be responsible for our actions. By recognizing the importance of self-care and setting clear boundaries, we can create a life that is fulfilling, balanced, and aligned with our true selves. So, let us embark on this journey of personal accountability, embracing the power it holds to transform our lives for the better.

Celebrating Your Achievements and Progress

Subchapter: Celebrating Your Achievements and Progress

Introduction:

In our journey towards personal accountability, it is crucial to recognize and celebrate our achievements and progress. Taking responsibility for our actions involves acknowledging the positive outcomes we have contributed to and the growth we have experienced. By embracing these celebrations, we can fuel our motivation, enhance our self-confidence, and reinforce the importance of personal accountability. This subchapter explores the significance of celebrating achievements and progress in our lives.

1. The Power of Acknowledgment: One of the key aspects of taking responsibility for our actions is recognizing and acknowledging the milestones we have reached. By acknowledging our achievements, we affirm our ability to overcome challenges and make a positive impact. Celebrating even the smallest victories motivates us to continue striving for personal growth and accountability.

2. Cultivating a Positive Mindset: Celebrating achievements helps us cultivate a positive mindset by shifting our focus from shortcomings to accomplishments. It allows us to appreciate the progress we have made and encourages us to persevere during challenging times. By celebrating our achievements, we reinforce the belief that we are capable of taking control of our lives.

3. Building Self-Confidence:
Regularly celebrating our achievements boosts our self-confidence. It reminds us of our capabilities and affirms that our efforts are not in vain. Recognizing our progress instills a sense of pride and belief in ourselves, empowering us to take on new challenges with courage and determination.

4. Inspiring Others:
When we celebrate our achievements, we inspire others to take responsibility for their own actions. Our celebrations serve as a testament to the power of personal accountability, encouraging others to believe in their potential and take steps towards their goals. By sharing our successes and progress, we create a ripple effect of positivity and accountability.

5. Embracing Gratitude:
Celebrating achievements and progress encourages us to practice gratitude. It reminds us of the support and opportunities we have received along the way. Expressing gratitude not only fosters a sense of appreciation but also strengthens our relationships and connections with others.

Conclusion:
In the journey towards personal accountability, celebrating our achievements and progress is vital. It helps us cultivate a positive mindset, build self-confidence, inspire others, and embrace gratitude. By acknowledging our accomplishments, we reinforce the importance of taking responsibility for our actions and empower ourselves to continue growing. Let us celebrate each step forward, no matter how small, as we embrace the power of personal accountability in our lives.

Inspiring Others Through Your Accountability Journey

Taking responsibility for your actions is not only a powerful way to transform your own life, but it can also serve as a beacon of inspiration for others. When you demonstrate personal accountability, you become a role model for those around you, showing them the immense power that comes from taking control of your life. In this subchapter, we will explore how your accountability journey can inspire others and create a ripple effect of positive change.

One of the most profound ways to inspire others through your accountability journey is by leading by example. When people see you taking responsibility for your actions, they witness the transformative effects it has on your life. They observe your growth, resilience, and commitment to self-improvement. This can motivate them to examine their own lives and consider the positive impact personal accountability could have on their own journey.

Another way to inspire others is by sharing your story. People are often drawn to personal narratives of triumph over adversity. By openly discussing the challenges you have faced and how personal accountability helped you overcome them, you create a relatable and inspiring narrative. Your story can serve as a catalyst for change in the lives of others, showing them that they too have the power to take control and create a better future.

Additionally, practicing empathy and offering support to others can be a powerful way to influence their mindset towards personal accountability. By actively listening to their struggles and providing non-judgmental guidance, you can help them recognize their own patterns of behavior and the role they play in their outcomes. This encouragement can ignite a spark within them, motivating them to embark on their own accountability journey.

Lastly, celebrating the successes of others is crucial in inspiring them to continue their own accountability journey. By acknowledging and appreciating their progress, you reinforce the positive changes they have made. This recognition can fuel their motivation and encourage them to keep pushing forward, knowing that their efforts are seen and appreciated.

In conclusion, taking responsibility for your actions can inspire others in profound ways. By leading by example, sharing your story, offering support, and celebrating their successes, you can create a ripple effect of positive change. Remember, your accountability journey is not just about personal growth; it has the power to inspire and uplift those around you. Embrace this opportunity to inspire others and create a world where personal accountability is valued and celebrated by everyone.

Chapter 10: Sustaining Personal Accountability in the Long Run

Developing a Supportive Network

In the journey of personal accountability, it is crucial to recognize the significance of developing a supportive network. Surrounding oneself with like-minded individuals who share the same values and goals can greatly enhance the process of taking responsibility for one's actions. This subchapter focuses on the importance of building a strong support system and provides practical tips on how to do so.

Taking responsibility for our actions requires a certain level of self-awareness and a willingness to grow. It is not an easy task to hold ourselves accountable and make positive changes alone. Having a supportive network can make this process more manageable and even enjoyable.

Firstly, it is important to evaluate our current relationships and determine whether they contribute to our accountability journey or hinder it. Surrounding ourselves with individuals who constantly blame others or avoid taking responsibility for their actions can derail our progress. Instead, we should seek out individuals who inspire and challenge us to be better versions of ourselves.

One effective way to develop a supportive network is by joining accountability groups or communities. These can be found both in-person and online, catering to various interests and goals. Engaging with others who are also on a journey of personal accountability can provide valuable insights, encouragement, and support. It creates an environment where individuals can share their experiences, learn from one another, and hold each other accountable.

In addition to joining existing groups, it is also essential to actively seek out individuals who share similar values and goals. This may involve attending workshops, seminars, or networking events focused on personal growth and accountability. By connecting with like-minded individuals, we can expand our support system and build meaningful relationships that foster personal development.

Furthermore, it is crucial to remember that a supportive network is a two-way street. We must be willing to offer our support and encouragement to others as well. By actively participating in the growth and development of our network, we contribute to the overall success and well-being of everyone involved.

In conclusion, developing a supportive network is an integral part of taking responsibility for our actions. Surrounding ourselves with individuals who share similar values and goals can greatly enhance our accountability journey. By evaluating existing relationships, joining accountability groups, seeking out like-minded individuals, and actively participating in the growth of the network, we can create an environment that fosters personal development and empowers everyone involved. Remember, together we can achieve more than we can alone.

Reflecting on Your Accountability Journey

In the journey of personal growth and self-improvement, one of the most powerful tools we can possess is the ability to take responsibility for our actions. It is in this acknowledgment of our own accountability that we find the true power to transform our lives and achieve our goals. In this subchapter, we will delve into the importance of reflecting on your accountability journey and how it can lead you to a more fulfilling and successful life.

Taking responsibility for your actions is not always an easy task. It requires a deep level of self-awareness and a willingness to acknowledge your mistakes and shortcomings. However, it is through this process that you gain the power to change and grow. Reflecting on your accountability journey allows you to examine your actions, decisions, and choices, and evaluate how they have impacted your life and the lives of those around you.

By reflecting on your accountability journey, you can identify patterns and behaviors that may be hindering your progress. You can uncover areas where you have fallen short and take steps to rectify them. This self-reflection helps you understand the consequences of your actions and empowers you to make better choices in the future.

Moreover, reflecting on your accountability journey allows you to celebrate your successes and milestones. It is important to acknowledge and appreciate the progress you have made. By recognizing your achievements, big or small, you can boost your self-confidence and motivation to continue on your path of personal accountability.

In this subchapter, we will provide you with practical exercises and techniques to facilitate your reflection process. We will guide you through various methods of self-assessment and encourage you to analyze your thoughts, emotions, and behaviors. We will help you identify areas where you can improve and provide strategies to hold yourself accountable moving forward.

Remember, personal accountability is not a destination but a lifelong journey. It requires constant self-reflection and a commitment to growth. By reflecting on your accountability journey, you embrace the power to take control of your life and manifest your true potential.

Whether you are just beginning your journey of personal accountability or have been on this path for some time, this subchapter will provide valuable insights and guidance to help you continue your growth. So, let us embark on this journey together and discover the transformative power of reflecting on your accountability.

Continuously Reinforcing and Strengthening Your Accountability Skills

In today's fast-paced world, it is easy to get caught up in the whirlwind of life and lose sight of one crucial aspect: personal accountability. Taking responsibility for our actions is not only a sign of maturity and integrity, but it also empowers us to take control of our lives and shape our future. In this subchapter, we will explore the importance of continuously reinforcing and strengthening your accountability skills, regardless of your background or current circumstances.

Accountability is not a one-time event; it is a lifelong process that requires dedication and commitment. Just as we exercise to keep our bodies fit, we must exercise our accountability skills regularly to keep them sharp and effective. By doing so, we become more reliable, trustworthy, and respected individuals.

One way to reinforce your accountability skills is by setting realistic goals for yourself. By setting clear and measurable objectives, you create a roadmap for success and hold yourself accountable for achieving them. Regularly reviewing your progress and making necessary adjustments will ensure that you stay on track, fostering a sense of personal responsibility.

Another essential aspect of accountability is owning up to your mistakes. Rather than deflecting blame or making excuses, embrace the opportunity to learn and grow from your errors. By acknowledging your role in any situation, you demonstrate humility and foster trust with those around you.

To strengthen your accountability skills further, seek feedback from others. Actively listen to their perspectives, whether it is constructive criticism or praise, and reflect on how you can improve. Surrounding yourself with individuals who value accountability will inspire and motivate you to be better.

Furthermore, accountability extends beyond personal responsibility; it also encompasses taking ownership of the impact you have on others. Being mindful of your interactions and the consequences of your actions is crucial for creating positive relationships and fostering a supportive environment.

Lastly, continuously reinforcing and strengthening your accountability skills requires self-reflection and self-awareness. Take the time to analyze your thoughts, emotions, and behaviors. Identify any patterns or tendencies that hinder your accountability and work on developing strategies to overcome them.

In conclusion, taking responsibility for your actions is a fundamental aspect of personal accountability. By continuously reinforcing and strengthening your accountability skills, you empower yourself to take control of your life and create a positive impact on those around you. Remember, accountability is not a destination but a lifelong journey. So, embrace it, cultivate it, and watch as it transforms your life for the better.

Conclusion: Embracing Personal Accountability as a Path to Success and Fulfillment

In today's fast-paced and ever-changing world, it is easy to get caught up in the blame game. We often find ourselves pointing fingers at others or external circumstances when things don't go our way. However, the key to unlocking true success and fulfillment lies in embracing personal accountability.

Taking responsibility for your actions is essential for growth and development. It is about acknowledging that you have the power to shape your own destiny and make choices that align with your values and goals. By embracing personal accountability, you are taking control of your life and refusing to be a victim of circumstances.

When you take ownership of your actions, you become proactive. You stop waiting for things to happen and start making them happen. This mindset shift opens up a world of opportunities and possibilities. Instead of feeling helpless, you become empowered to take the necessary steps to achieve your dreams.

Personal accountability also fosters resilience. It allows you to bounce back from setbacks and failures, viewing them as learning experiences rather than roadblocks. When you take responsibility for your actions, you understand that mistakes are an inevitable part of the journey to success. Rather than dwelling on them, you learn from them and move forward with renewed determination.

Furthermore, embracing personal accountability builds trust and credibility. When you consistently demonstrate that you are reliable and dependable, others will have confidence in your abilities. Whether it is in personal relationships, professional settings, or any other aspect of life, people gravitate towards individuals who take responsibility for their actions. By doing so, you inspire others to do the same, creating a positive ripple effect in your community.

In conclusion, personal accountability is not just a mindset; it is a way of life. By taking responsibility for your actions, you seize control of your destiny, foster growth, and build resilience. Embracing personal accountability enables you to overcome obstacles, learn from failures, and grow into the best version of yourself.

So, dear reader, I invite you to make a commitment to personal accountability. Embrace the power within you to shape your life and take responsibility for your actions. Remember, success and fulfillment are not handed to us; they are earned through hard work, perseverance, and personal accountability. Begin your journey today and unlock the limitless potential that lies within you.